SECOND EDITION 0

Student's Book

SUPER MINDS

Herbert Puchta · Peter Lewis-Jones

CAMBRIDGE
UNIVERSITY PRESS

Map of the Book

Say *Hello!* (pages 4–9)

Vocabulary	Language Focus	Story	
Colors Numbers 1 – 10	• *Hello! What's your name?* • *I'm …* • *What color is it?*	**Story** *Friends* **Value** Making Friends	

▶ Song: Let's Be Friends

1 My Classroom (pages 10–19)

What's in my classroom?

Vocabulary	Language Focus	Story	Think and Learn
Classroom Objects	• Imperatives • *What is it? It's …*	*The Butterfly* **Value** Appreciating Nature	Math: Patterns

▶ Song: Look! It's My Classroom ▶ Creativity: Create That! ▶ Review: Think Back

2 My Body (pages 20–29)

How do we move?

Vocabulary	Language Focus	Story	Think and Learn
The Body	• *I have …* • *How many … ?*	*Great Costumes!* **Value** Using Your Imagination	Science: Our Skeleton

▶ Song: Run, Run, Run! ▶ Creativity: Do That! ▶ Review: Think Back

3 My Family (pages 30–39)

What's a family?

Vocabulary	Language Focus	Story	Think and Learn
Family	• *This is my …* • *Is this your … ?*	*Cool Grandma* **Value** Appreciating Family	Social Science: An Animal Family

▶ Song: A Nice Family ▶ Creativity: Create That! ▶ Review: Think Back

4 At the Zoo (pages 40–49)

Where can we find animals?

Vocabulary	Language Focus	Story	Think and Learn
Animals	• Adjectives • *What's your favorite … ?*	*My Favorite Animal* **Value** Friendship	Science: Animal Habitats

▶ Song: Where Are the Animals? ▶ Creativity: Do That! ▶ Review: Think Back

5 My Food (pages 50–59)

What food do we eat?

Vocabulary	Language Focus	Story	Think and Learn
Food	• *I like / I don't like …* • *Do you like … ?*	*The Cupcakes* **Value** Sharing	Science: Fruit and Vegetables

▶ Song: I Like You ▶ Creativity: Create That! ▶ Review: Think Back

6 My Town (pages 60–69)

What's in your town?

Vocabulary	Language Focus	Story	Think and Learn
Places in a Town	• *There's / There are …* • *Where's the … ? It's there.*	*The Toy Store* **Value** Being Kind	Geography: Maps and Towns

▶ Song: A Really Cool Town ▶ Creativity: Do That! ▶ Review: Think Back

7 Jobs (pages 70–79)

What's a job?

Vocabulary	Language Focus	Story	Think and Learn
Jobs	• *He's/She's a …* • *Is he/she a … ?*	*The Teacher* **Value** Appreciating Others	Social Science: Inside and Outside Jobs

▶ Song: Helping Me, Helping You ▶ Creativity: Create That! ▶ Review: Think Back

8 My Clothes (pages 80–89)

What clothes do we need?

Vocabulary	Language Focus	Story	Think and Learn
Clothes	• *I'm wearing …* • *Is he/she wearing … ?*	*Hot or Cold?* **Value** Being Prepared	Science: Different Clothes

Song: It's Cold! ▶ Creativity: Do That! ▶ Review: Think Back

9 My Hobbies (pages 90–99)

What are hobbies?

Vocabulary	Language Focus	Story	Think and Learn
Hobbies	• *I'm + ing* • *Are you + ing?*	*Guess What I'm Doing?* **Value** Saying Sorry	Math: Bar Charts

Song: I'm Having Fun ▶ Creativity: Create That! ▶ Review: Think Back

Practice of Creative Thinking, Critical Thinking, and Cognitive Skills

Say Hello!

1 01 Listen and sing.

1 03 Listen and point. Say the names.

2 Ask and answer.

1 04 Listen and point. Listen and say the words.

2 Look and find. Say.

1 05 Listen and point. Listen and say the numbers.

2 Point and say. Count.

Friends

1 06 Watch and listen to the story.

2 Find and color. Say the colors.

1 My Classroom

1 07 Listen and point. Say the words.

BIG QUESTION What's in my classroom?

2 08 Listen and chant.

1 09 Listen and point. Listen and stick.

1 

2 

3 

4 

2 10 Look, listen, and say.

3 Work with a partner. Say and do.

1 11 Listen and sing.

2 Count the classroom objects and the children.

1 Listen and circle. (13)

1

2

3

4

2 Watch and listen.

3 Play the game.

The Butterfly

1 14 Watch and listen to the story.

2 What's different? Look and circle.

Think and Learn

PATTERNS

Watch and listen.

1 15 Listen and point.

1 
crayon

2 
pen

3 
eraser

2 Point and say the numbers.

1 2 3 4 5 ? 7 8 ? 10

1 2 3 ? 5 6 7 ? 9 10

3 16 Say what's next. Listen and check.

1  ?

2  ?

3  ?

4 Choose and circle the next picture.

1 

2 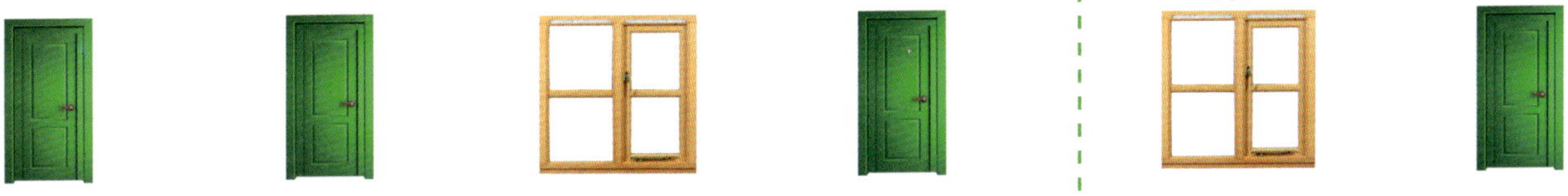

3 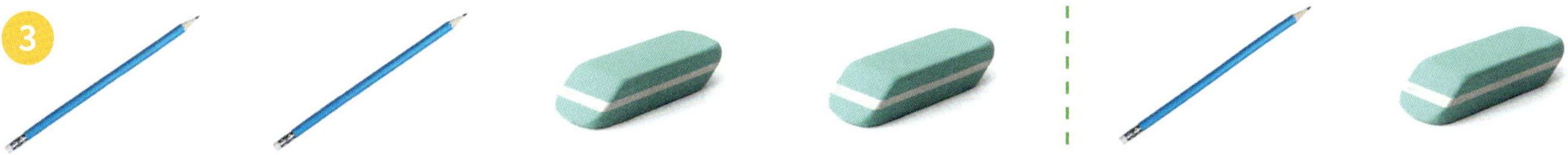

4 

5 Project Create your own pattern. Say.

Create That!

1 17 Listen and imagine.
Then draw your picture.

2 Show your picture to your friend. Say.

1 (18) Listen and point. Then say.

2 (19) Listen and circle.

1 

2 

3 

4 

3 Draw the last picture.

1 

2 

2 My Body

1 🎧 20 Listen and point. Say the words.

BIG QUESTION How do we move?

2 🎧 21 Listen and chant.

1 22 Listen to the monsters. Color.

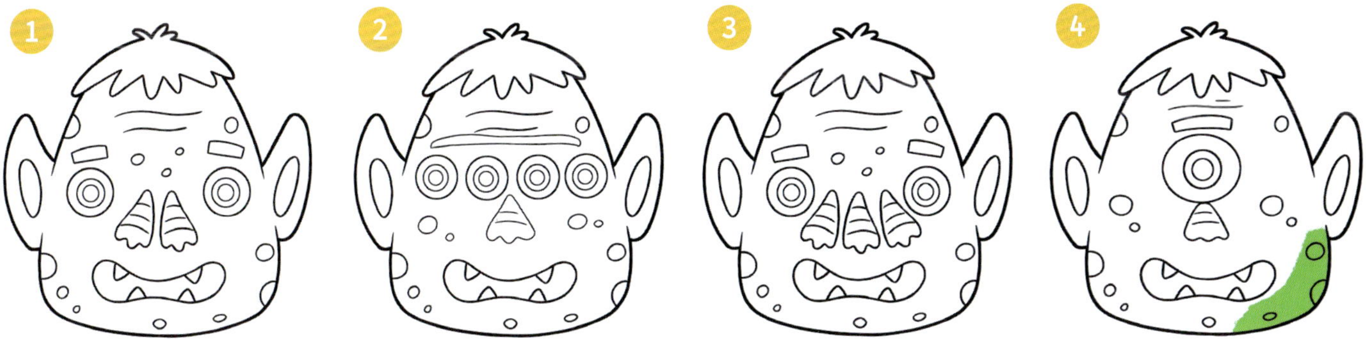

2 23 Look, listen, and say.

3 Play the monster game.

1 24 Listen and sing.

2 Which monster? Say *chocolate* or *ice cream*.

1

2

3

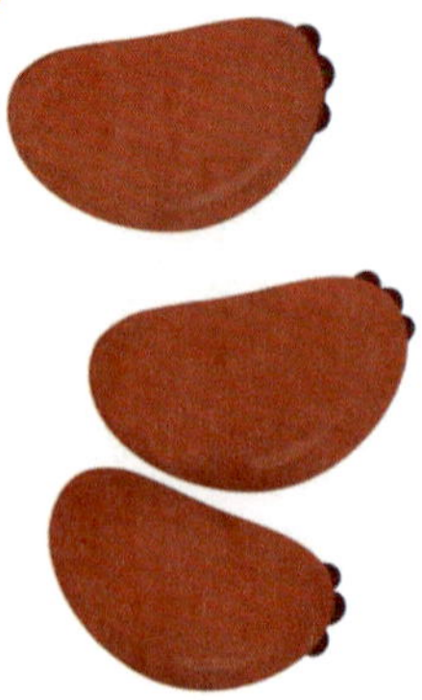

4

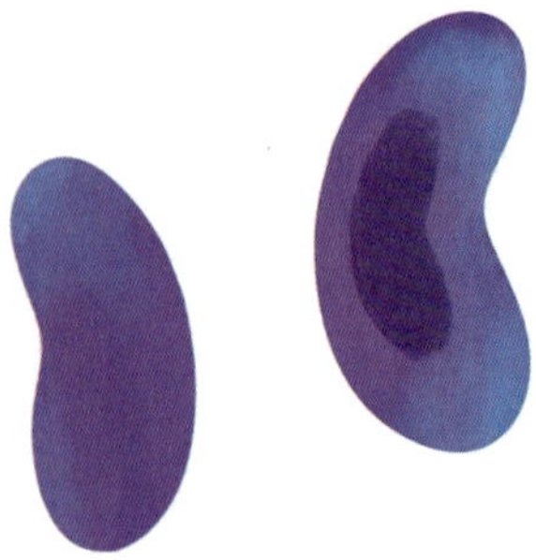

1 26 Listen and draw.

2 Watch and listen.

3 Draw a monster. Play *Ask the Monster*.

Great Costumes!

1 27 Watch and listen to the story.

7

8

2 Find, count, and stick.

1

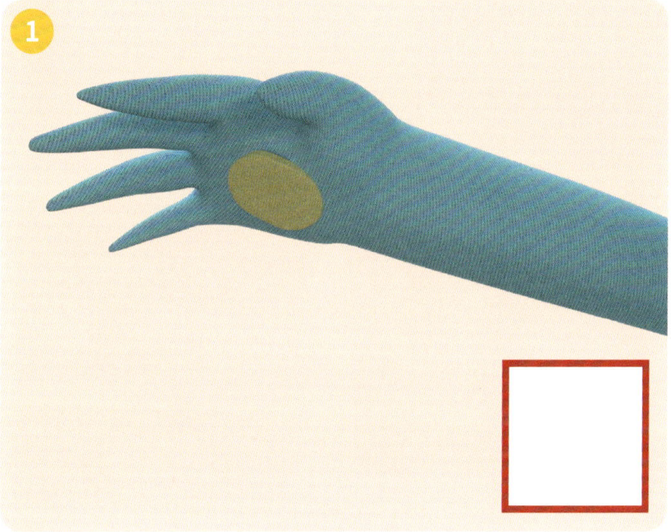

2

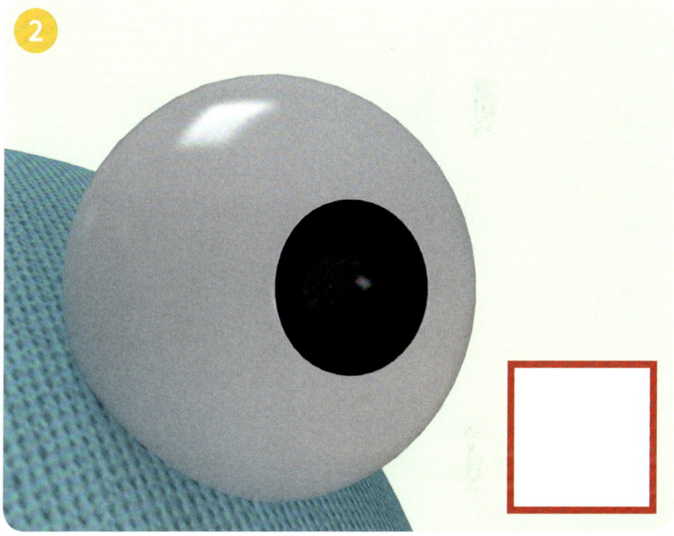

3

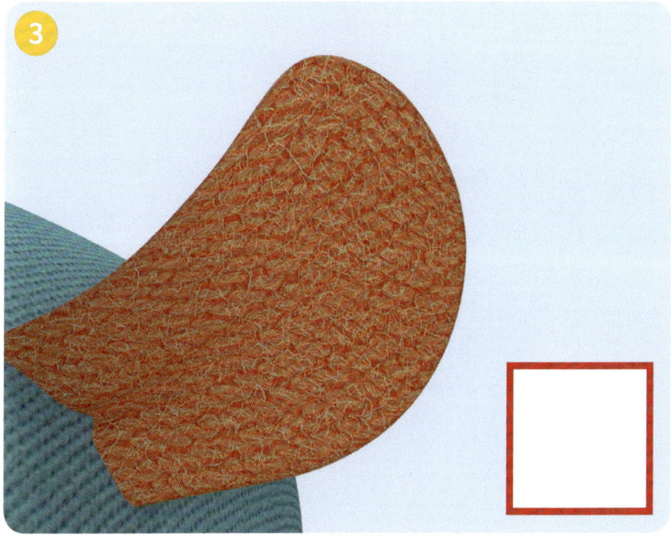

4

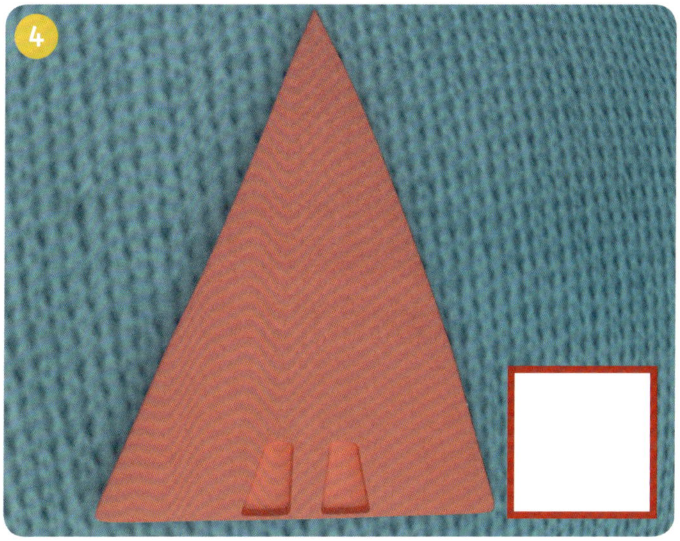

OUR SKELETON

Watch and listen.

1 28 Listen and point.

1

walk

2

run

3

wave

2 Look and match.

1

2

3

4

a

b
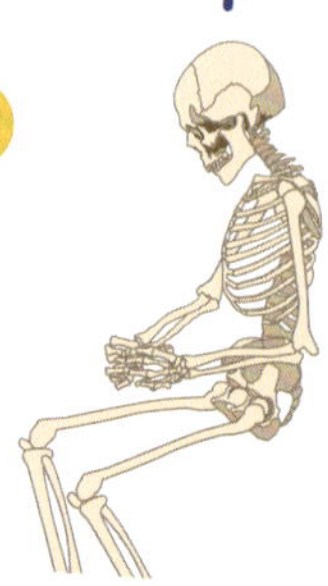

c
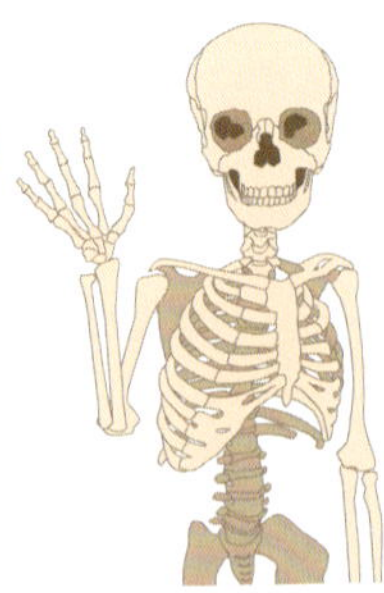

d
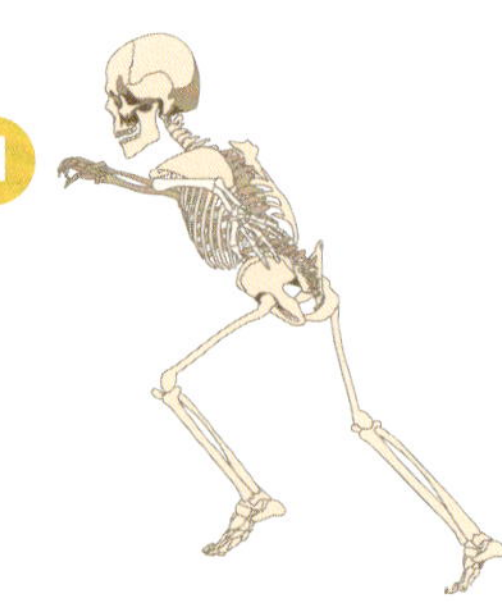

3 Look and say.

1

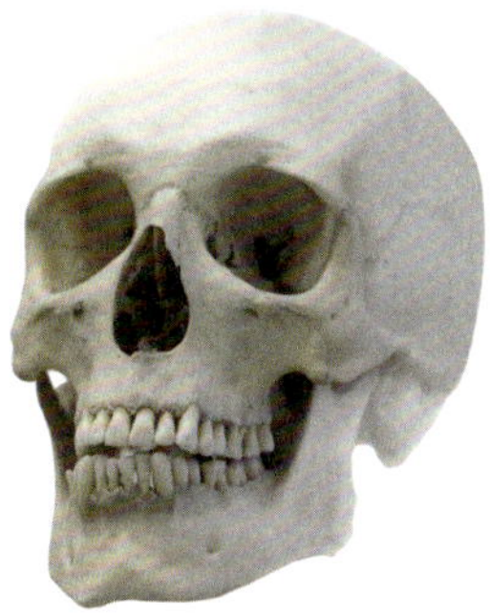

2

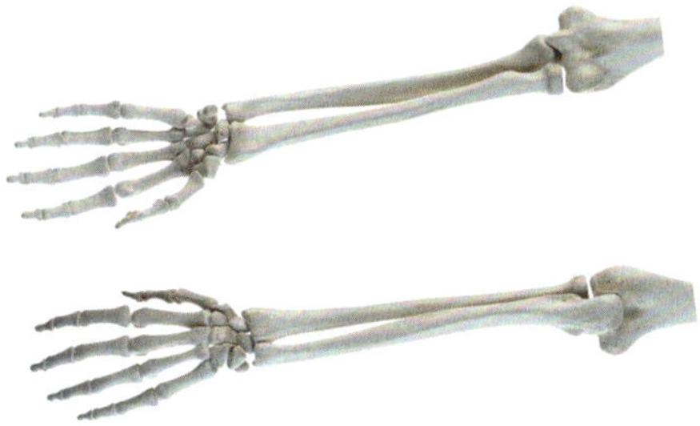

3

4

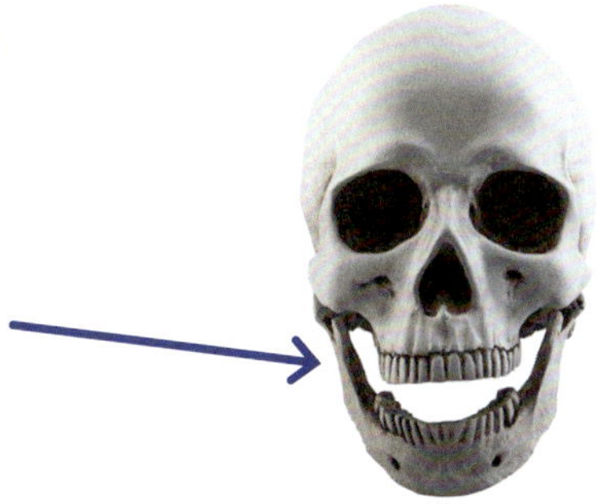

4 Project Draw three stick people.
Show how they run, wave, and sit.

1 Listen and act it out with your teacher. Then listen again and match.

1 2 3 4 5 6

1 30 Listen and point. Then say.

2 31 Listen and color.

3 Look and circle. Then say.

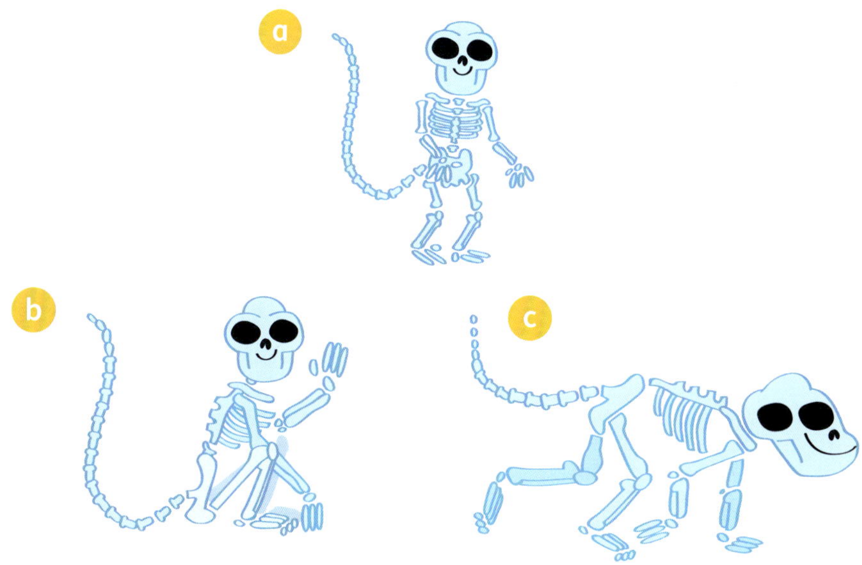

3 My Family

1 (32) Listen and point. Say the words.

BIG QUESTION What's a family?

2 (33) Listen and chant.

1 (34) Listen and circle the correct person.

1

2

3

4

2 (35) Look, listen, and say.

3 Draw your family. Point and say.

1 36 Listen and sing.

2 How many in each family? Look and count.

1 38 Listen and stick.

2 Watch and listen.

3 Ask and answer.

Cool Grandma

1 39 Watch and listen to the story.

7

8

2 Find and count. Draw how many.

An Animal Family

▶ Watch and listen.

1 40 Listen and point.

1

chicken

2

dog

3

duck

4

cat

2 Look and match.

1

2

3

4

3 Look and circle the different animal.

1

2

3

4 Project Make an animal family. Say.

1 41 Listen and imagine.
Then draw your picture.

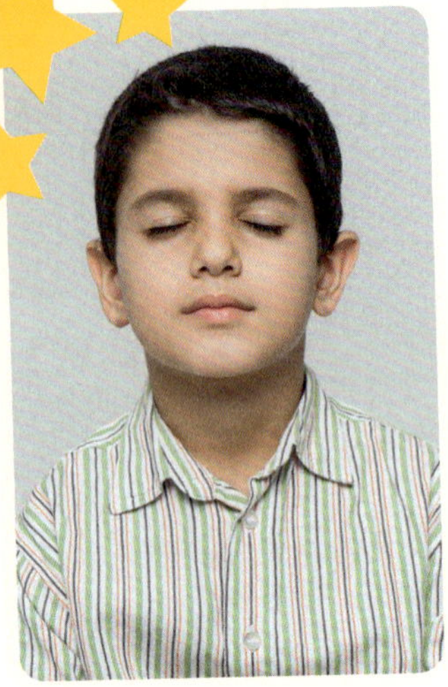

2 Show your picture to your friend. Say.

1 42 Listen and point. Then say.

2 43 Listen and color.

3 Look and circle the different animal.

4 At the Zoo

1 44 Listen and point. Say the words.

BIG QUESTION Where can we find animals?

2 45 Listen and chant.

1 46 Listen and stick.

1

2

3

4

5

6

2 47 Look, listen, and say.

3 Complete the pictures. Point and say.

1

2

3

4

1 48 Listen and sing.

2 Find and circle the four animals in the song.

1 50 Listen and check ☑.

2 Watch and listen.

3 Draw for you. Then ask and answer.

	You	Friend
Favorite animal? 		
Favorite color? 		

My Favorite Animal

1 51 Watch and listen to the story.

7

8

2 What's different? Look and circle.

1

2

3

4

Animal Habitats

▶ Watch and listen.

1 🎧 52 Listen and point.

1

monkey

2

frog

3

tree

4

pond

5

grassland

2 Where do these animals live? Draw lines.

1

2

3

a

b

c

4

5

6

3 Look and circle the wrong animal.

a

b

c

4 Project Make a puzzle for your friend.

Do That!

1 53 Listen and act it out with your teacher. Then listen again and match.

1 2 3 4 5 6

1 54 Listen and point. Then say.

2 55 Listen and number.

a  ☐

b  ☐

c  ☐

d  1

3 Draw the missing animal. Then say.

1 

2 

5 My Food

1 56 Listen and point. Say the words.

BIG QUESTION What food do we eat?

2 57 Listen and chant.

1 58 Listen and stick 😊 or 😔.

1

2

3

4

5

6

2 59 Look, listen, and say.

3 Talk about food.

cupcake

tomatoes

milk

oranges

chocolate

pears

1 60 Listen and sing.

2 Look, think, and draw 😊 or 😔.

1 (62) Listen and draw 😊 or 😞.

2 Watch and listen.

3 Ask and answer. Draw 😊 or 😞.

	Me	My Friend ______	My Friend ______
pink			
blue			
green			
pears			
chocolate			
tomatoes			

1 63 Watch and listen to the story.

2 Look and draw the cupcakes.

Think and Learn

Fruit and Vegetables

Watch and listen.

1 64 Listen and point.

potatoes

carrots

bananas

ground

2 Where does our food come from? Draw lines.

3 Look and circle the wrong one.

1

2

4 Project Make a food picture. Say.

1 65 Listen and imagine. Then draw your picture.

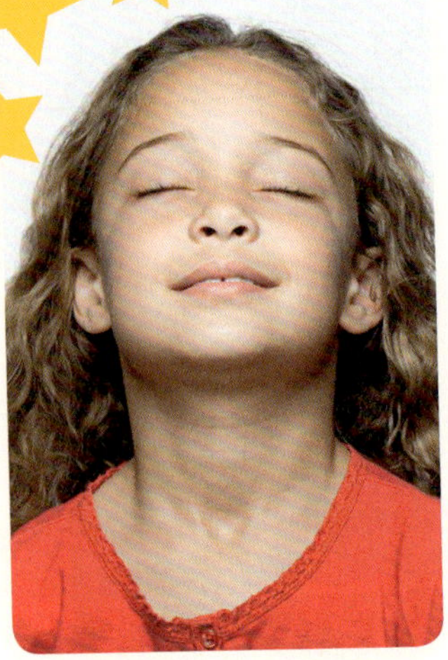

2 Show your plate to your friend. Say.

1 Read and match.

1 

2 

3 

pear

cupcake

orange

2 Read and draw or .

1 

I don't like cake.

2 

Do you like chocolate?

Yes, I do.

3 Which food is different? Circle.

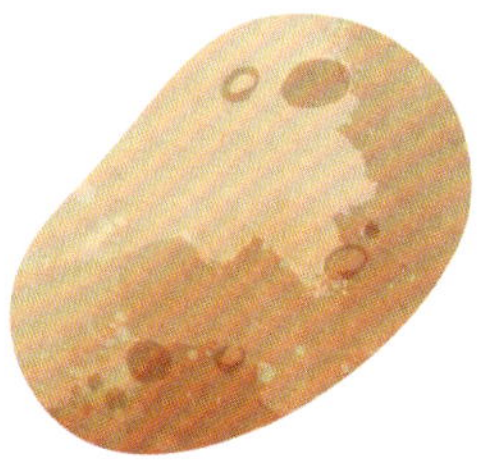

6 My Town

1 66 Listen and point. Say the words.

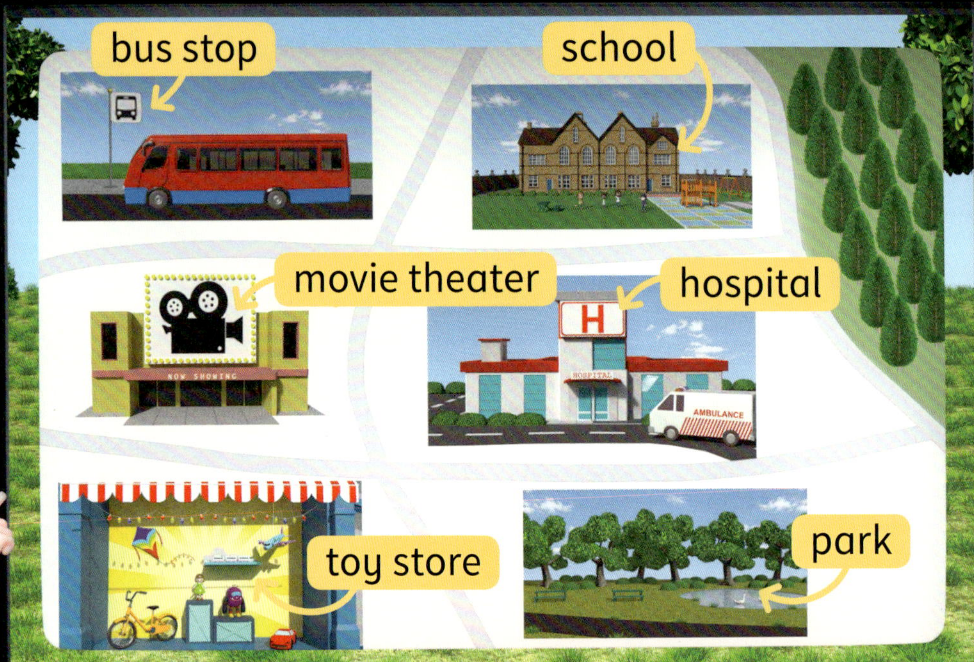

BIG QUESTION What's in your town?

2 67 Listen and chant.

1 68 Listen and match.

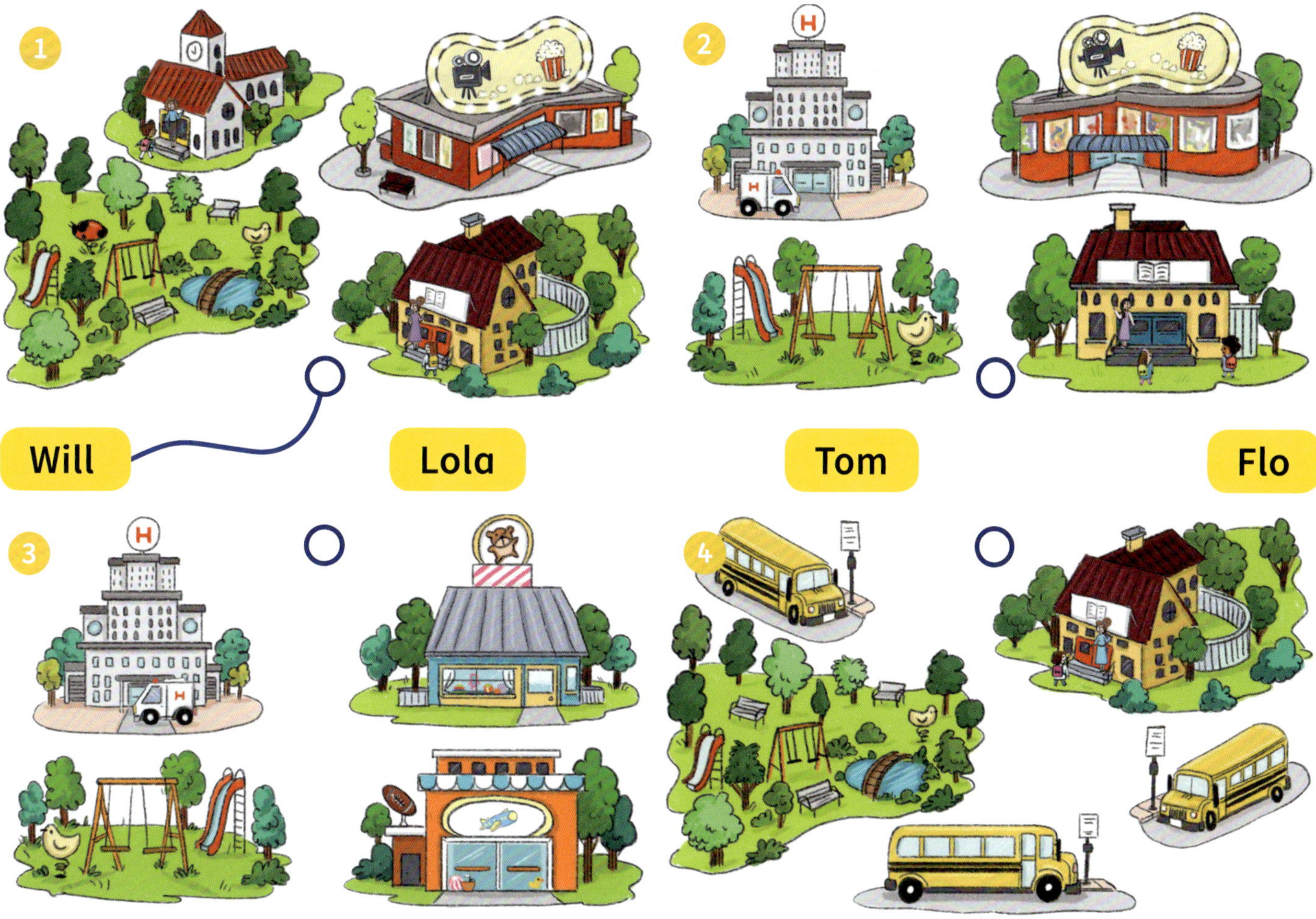

2 69 Look, listen, and say.

3 Draw your town. Say.

1 70 Listen and sing.

2 Where do these people work? Point and say.

1 

2 

3 

4 

1 (72) Listen and draw Max's route.

2 Watch and listen.

3 Ask a partner. Find and answer.

pear cake lion milk book pencil

The Toy Store

1 73 Watch and listen to the story.

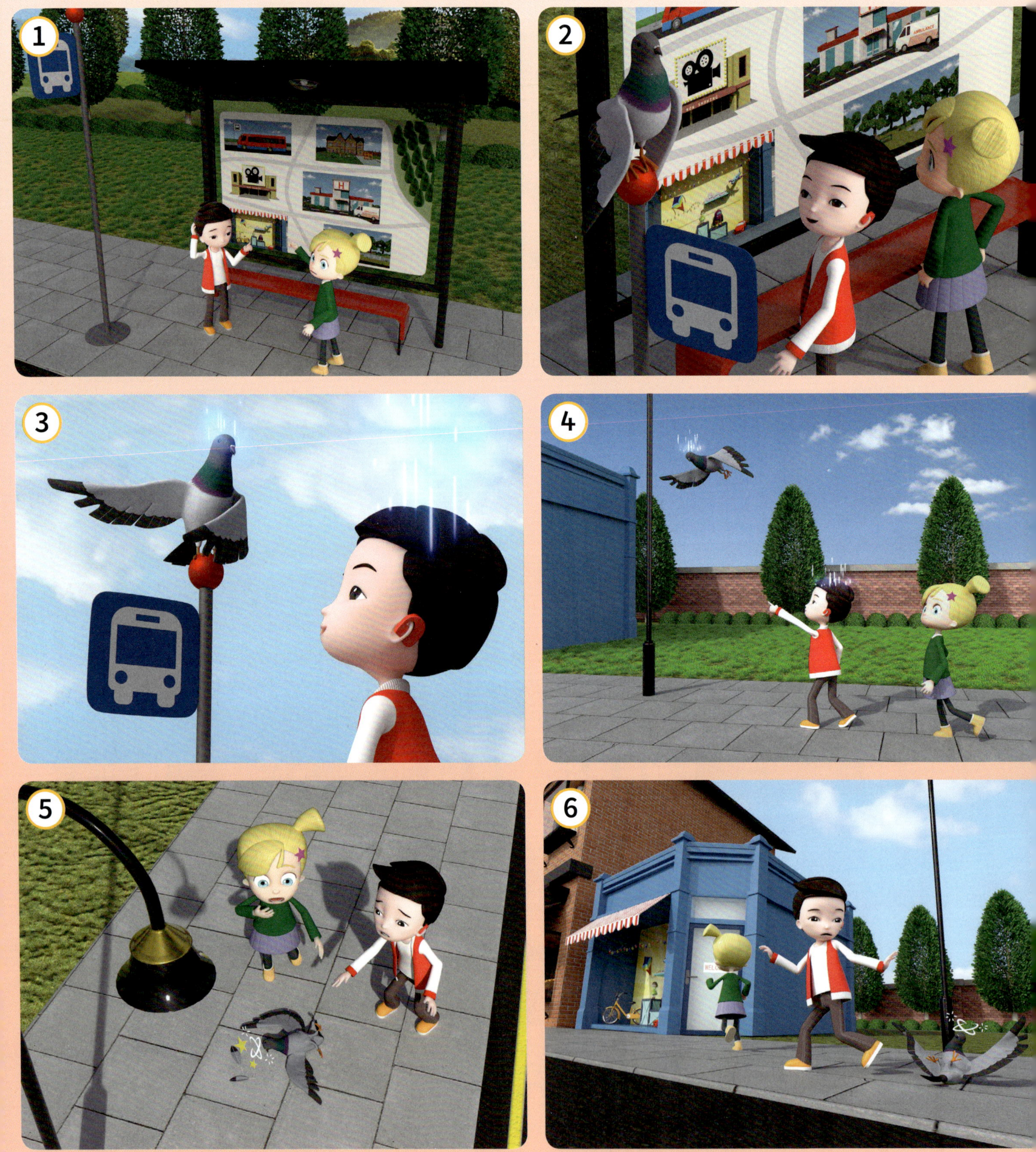

2 Look, find, and write the picture number.

a

6

b

c

d

e

f

Maps and Towns

Watch and listen.

1 74 Listen and point.

1 market

2 café

3 playground

4 sports center
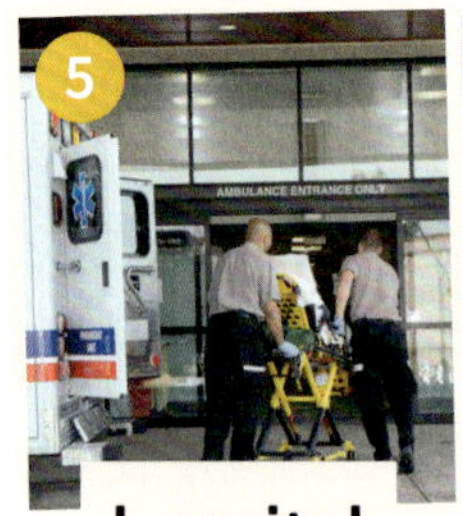
5 hospital

6 movie theater

2 Look and match. Write the numbers.

a 4
b
c
d
e
f

3 Look and stick.

4 Draw symbols. Then say.

5 Project Make a map of your dream town.

Look! There are two movie theaters!

1 75 Listen and act it out with your teacher. Listen again and match.

1 2 3 4 5 6

1 Read and match.

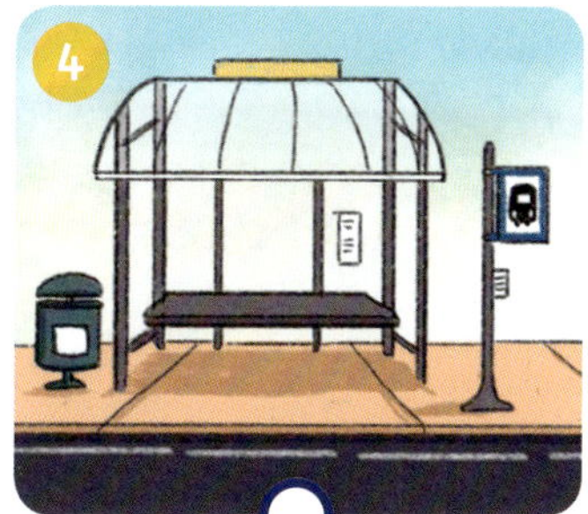

toy store | movie theater | bus stop | school

2 Write.

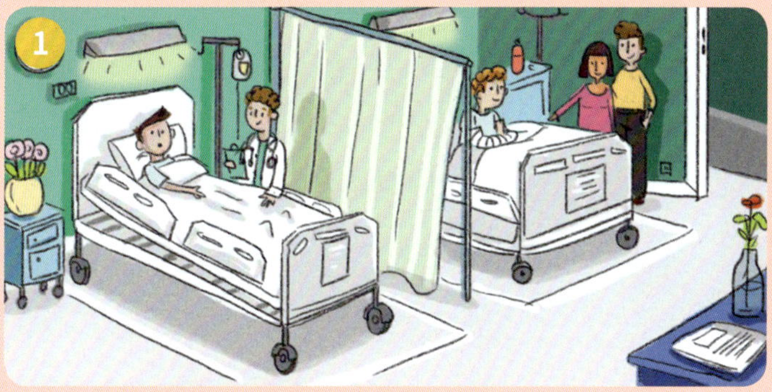

This is a ___ospital.

This is a ___ark.

3 Read and check ☑ or put an X ☒.

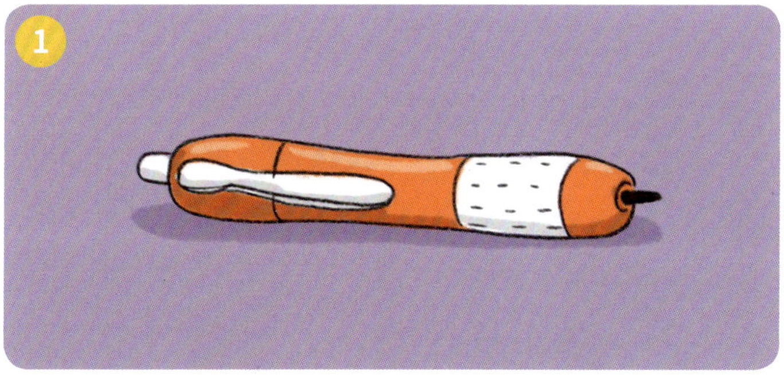

There's a pen. ☐

There are pen. ☐

There's four pens. ☐

There are four pens. ☐

7 Jobs

1 76 Listen and point. Say the words.

BIG QUESTION What's a job?

2 77 Listen and chant.

1 (78) Listen and check ☑.

2 (79) Look, listen, and say.

3 Look and draw lines. Say.

He's a police officer.

1 80 Listen and sing.

2 Mime a job for your partner to guess. Wave and say *Hello* if they're correct!

1 82 Listen, read, and check ☑.

- [ ] doctor
- [x] gardener

- [ ] teacher
- [ ] doctor

- [ ] firefighter
- [ ] police officer

- [ ] firefighter
- [ ] vet

2 Watch and listen.

3 Point. Ask and answer.

Is she a vet?

Yes, she is.

The Teacher

1 83 Watch and listen to the story.

2 Look at picture 6. Circle four differences.

INSIDE AND OUTSIDE JOBS

Watch and listen.

1 84 Listen and point.

1 farmer

2 salesclerk

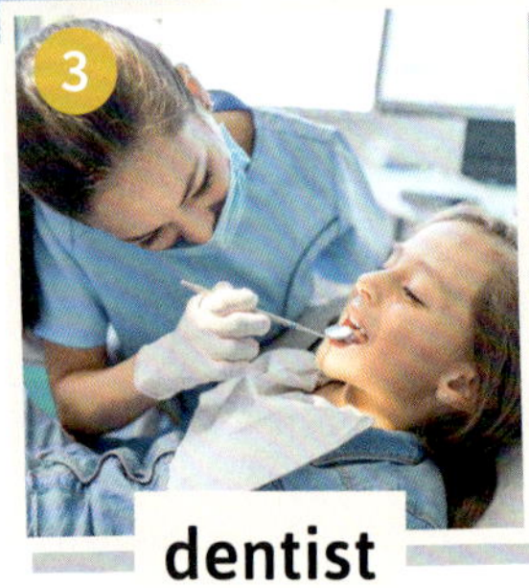
3 dentist

4 inside

5 outside

2 Look and stick.

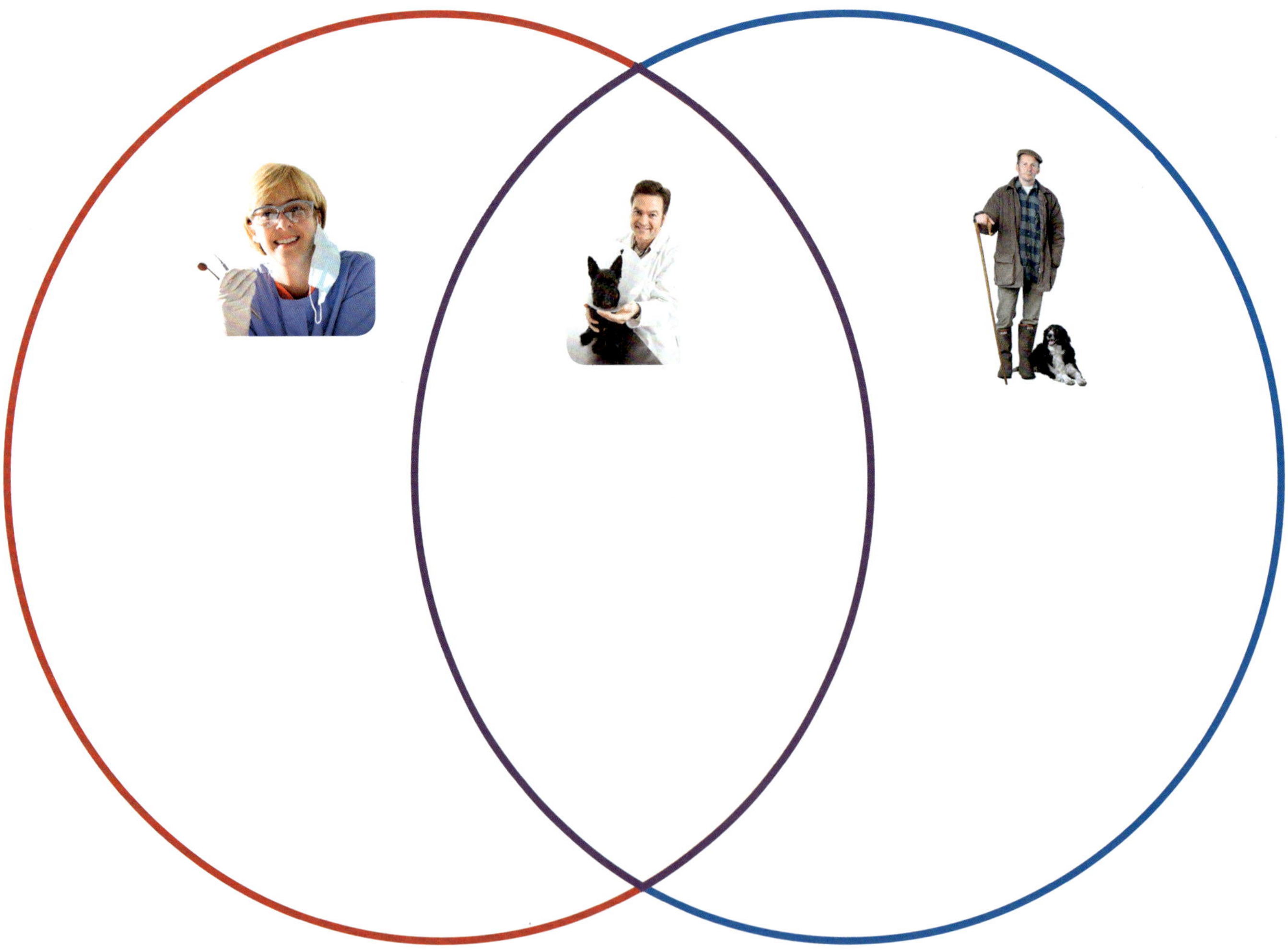

3 Where do they work? Look and write *I* for *inside*, *O* for *outside*, or *B* for *both*.

a

b

c

d

e

f

4 Project Make a class poster. Say.

He's a farmer.
He's outside.

1 85 Listen and imagine. Then draw your picture.

2 Show your picture to your friend. Say.

1 Read and match.

1 
2 
3 
4 

teacher | firefighter | police officer | doctor

2 Complete the words.

1 

She' s a ___ardener.

2 

___ ___'s a vet.

3 

___ ___ ___'s a ___irefighter.

3 Read and check ☑.

1 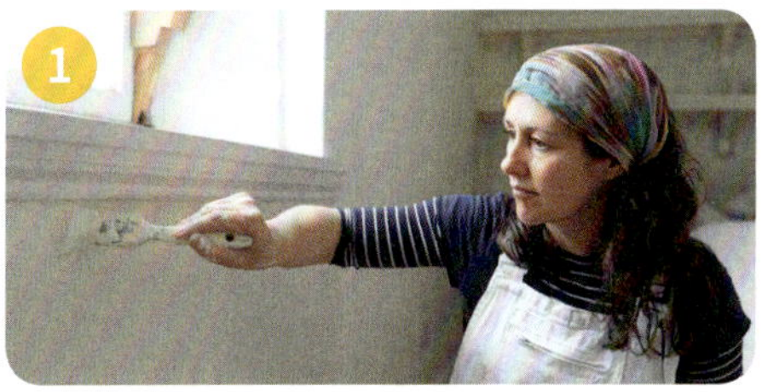

Is she a doctor?

Yes, she is. ☐

No, she isn't. ☐

2 

Is he a police officer?

Yes, he is. ☐

No, he isn't. ☐

3 

She's a …

police officer. ☐

teacher. ☐

8 My Clothes

1 86 Listen and point. Say the words.

BIG QUESTION What clothes do we need?

2 87 Listen and chant.

1 88 Listen and check ☑.

1
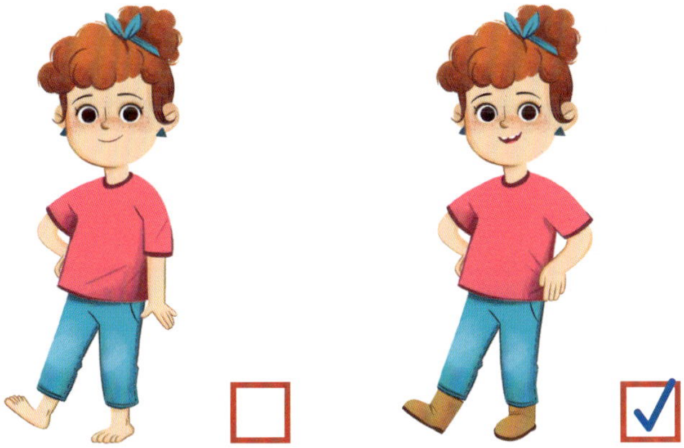

2

3

4

2 89 Look, listen, and say.

3 Choose and color your outfit. Say.

1 90 Listen and sing.

2 Read and number the clothes in order.

☐ scarf ☐ 1 jeans ☐ coat ☐ hat

1 92 Listen and stick.

Will

Fran

2 Watch and listen.

3 Work with a partner. Play *Guess Who?*

Is he wearing a scarf?

Yes, he is.

Ben

Alex

Tom

Jill

Eva

Ann

Hot or Cold?

1 93 Watch and listen to the story.

2 Look and read. Check ☑ Misty's clothes.

scarf				
jeans	✓			
coat				
hat				
sweater				
T-shirt				

Different Clothes

▶ Watch and listen.

1 🎧 94 Listen and point.

1 soft

2 hard

3 cold

4 hot

5 belt

6 sunglasses

2 Is it soft or hard? Draw lines.

1 

2 

3 

soft

hard

4 

5 

6 

3 Circle the items red for hot weather and blue for cold weather.

1 

2 

3 

4 

5 

6 

7 

8 

9 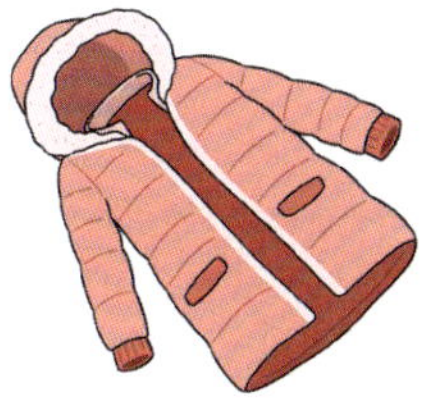

4 Project Draw clothes in a table.

	soft	hard
hot		
cold		

Do That!

1 95 Listen and act it out with your teacher. Listen again and match.

1 2 3 4 5 6

1 Read and match.

1 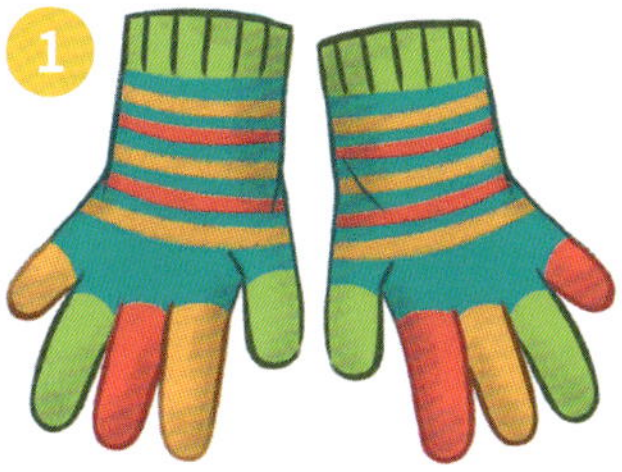

2 

3 

4 

coat gloves boots sweater

2 Listen and write *S* for *Sally*, *T* for *Tim*, and *K* for *Kate*.

96

1  ☐

2  ☐

3  ☐

3 Look and circle *soft* or *hard*.

1 

soft
hard

2 

soft
hard

3 

soft
hard

4 

soft
hard

9 My Hobbies

1 97 Listen and point. Say the words.

BIG QUESTION What are hobbies?

2 98 Listen and chant.

1 (99) Listen and number.

a 

b 

c 

d 

e 

f 

2 (100) Look, listen, and say.

3 What's next? Look, draw, and say.

I'm dancing!

1 

2 

3 

1 101 Listen and sing.

2 Read, count the children, and write the number.

How many children are …

reading?	2	running?	
painting?		swimming?	
dancing?		playing soccer?	

1 103 Listen and stick.

1

2

3

4

5

6

2 Watch and listen.

3 Play the game.

Are you dancing?

Yes, I am!

Guess What I'm Doing?

1 104 Watch and listen to the story.

2 Look and write the words. Check ☑ the activity from the story.

swim	~~dance~~	play soccer	read

1

☐

dance

2

☐

______

3

☐

______

4

☐

______

BAR CHARTS

Watch and listen.

1 105 Listen and point.

1

bar chart

2
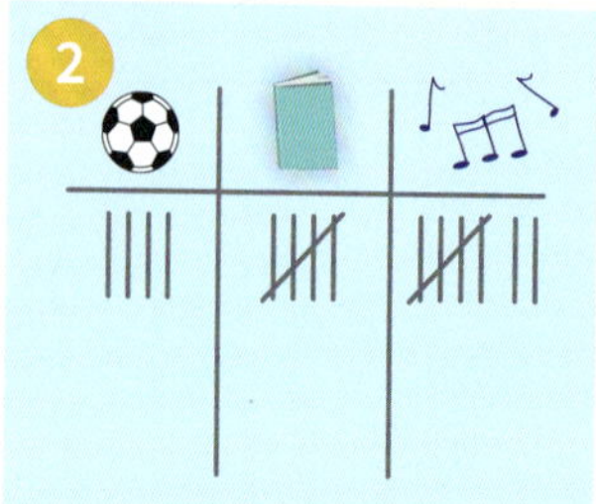
tally chart

3

computer games

4

movies

2 Look at the key and color the bar chart.

How many children like … ?

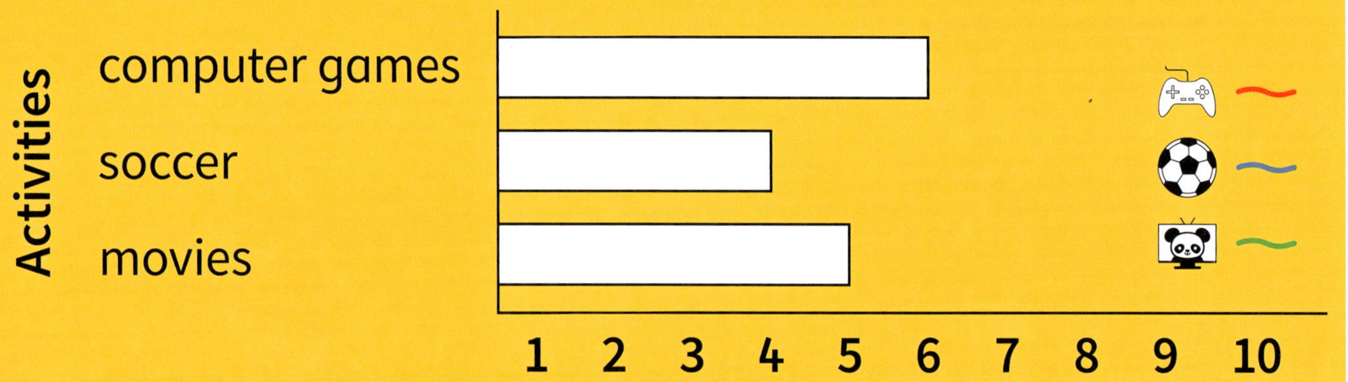

3 Look at the bar chart. Complete the tally chart.

Do you like …?	
playing soccer	IIII
watching movies	
playing computer games	

4 Project Make a bar chart about your friends.

a Ask questions and complete the tally chart:

Do you like reading?

Yes, I do.

Do you like ...?	
reading	
swimming	
dancing	

b Now draw a bar chart using the numbers on the tally chart.

c Color the bars.

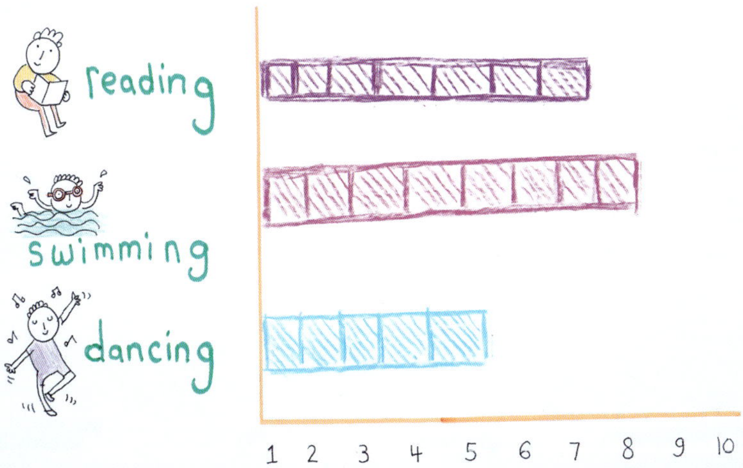

1 106 Listen and imagine. Then draw your picture.

2 Show your picture to your friend. Say.

Look! I'm playing soccer!

1 Read and match.

1 
2 
3 
4 

swim | play soccer | read | paint

2 Complete.

1 

__________ you running?
Yes, I am.

2 

Are you running?
No, __________ __________.

3 

Are you __________ soccer?
Yes, ________ ________.

3 Read and count. Write the numbers.

1 

☐

2 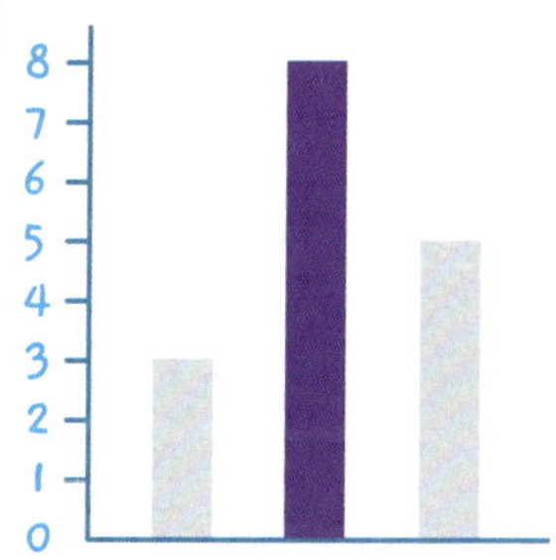

☐

3 

☐

The Alphabet

1 107 Look, listen, and say.

a b c d

j k l m

s t u v

e f g h i

n o p q r

w x y z

1 My Classroom

1 108 Look, listen, and say. Trace and color.

1

2

3

4

5

2 My Body

1 109 Look, listen, and say. Trace and color.

1

How many eyes do you have?

I have three eyes.

2

How many heads do you have?

I have two heads.

3

How many noses do you have?

I have five noses.

3 My Family

1 110 **Look, listen, and say. Trace and color.**

1

2

4 At the Zoo

1 111 Look, listen, and say. Trace and color.

1

2

5 My Food

1 112 Look, listen, and say. Draw 😊 or 😔.

6 My Town

1 113 **Look, listen, and say. Trace the words.**

1

There's a park.

2

There are two movie theaters.

3

Where's the park?

It's there.

4

Where's the movie theater?

It's there.

7 Jobs

1 114 Look, listen, and say. Trace the words.

1

Is he a firefighter?

No, he isn't. He's a gardener.

2

Is she a doctor?

No, she isn't. She's a gardener too.

8 My Clothes

1 115 **Look, listen, and say. Trace the words.**

1

Is he wearing a coat?

No, he isn't.

2

Is she wearing a scarf?

Yes, she is.

3

I'm wearing my hat!

9 My Hobbies

1 116 **Look, listen, and say. Trace the sentences.**

I'm swimming.

I'm running.

Are you running?

No, I'm not.

Are you dancing?

Yes, I am.

UNIT 1
page 11

UNIT 2
page 25

2 3 4 4

UNIT 3
page 33

UNIT 4
page 41

UNIT 5
page 51

UNIT 6
page 66

UNIT 7
page 76

page 83

page 93